The Easter Story

retold by **Allia Zobel Nolan**
illustrated by **Trace Moroney**

This book belongs to

This is the story of Easter, taken from Mark, chapters 11–16.
It tells the story of how much Jesus loves us, and teaches us how Jesus
gave his life for us, so that we could one day live with him in heaven.

Published by Kregel Kidzone,
an imprint of Kregel Publications
P.O. Box 2607, Grand Rapids, MI 49501

"You are looking for Jesus from Nazareth, the one who was killed on a cross. He has risen from death. He is not here."

Mark 16:6 ICB

While Jesus was on earth, he healed the sick and taught people about God. So everywhere he went, men and women, and boys and girls, wanted to meet him. One day, he had to go to Jerusalem to celebrate a feast day. As he rode into town on a donkey, a crowd ran out to meet him.

Some shouted, "Blessed is the king!" and put their coats down in his path. Others waved palm branches and sang songs. The leaders were jealous. They did not like Jesus. "Look how the people follow this man," they whispered. "We must find a way to get rid of him."

That night, Jesus ate the Passover Feast with his friends. He knew it would be the last meal they would eat together. He didn't want them to forget him. So when the food was passed around, he turned to them and said, "When you eat bread and drink wine like this, remember me."

Jesus knew the jealous leaders would take him
away soon. He also knew someone sitting in the
room would turn him in. "Who is it, Lord?" asked John.
Jesus answered, "The one I give bread to," as he passed
the loaf to Judas. Judas whispered an excuse and left.

After dinner, Jesus and some friends went to a garden. Jesus knew he would suffer and die so he was very sad. "I am going to pray now," Jesus said. "Please keep watch." His friends said, "Yes, Lord," but then they fell asleep.

Jesus knelt and closed his eyes. "Father, you can take away this cup of suffering that is to come," he said softly. "But I will do whatever you want." Then Jesus got up and went back to his friends.

Suddenly, a group of soldiers marched up to Jesus.
Judas was with them. He ran over to Jesus and
greeted him with a kiss. This was the signal for the
soldiers to arrest Jesus. And when they did, his
friends left him and ran away.

Jesus was brought before the leaders. Some people told lies about him. But they had no proof. So the leaders could not charge Jesus with any wrong. Then they asked, "You say you are the Son of God. Is that true?" Jesus answered, "I am." This made the leaders angry. "This man is guilty of a terrible offense. He says he is God's Son when he is not," they shouted. "For this, he must be punished."

The leaders decided Jesus must die on the cross. But first, he had to carry it a long way to a place called Calvary.

The cross was very heavy and Jesus fell three times. His friends could not do anything but look on and cry.

Jesus died soon after. His friends took his body and buried it in a new tomb. Then they rolled a big stone in front. But the leaders were still afraid.

They remembered that Jesus said he would rise again in three days.
So they gave an order for soldiers to guard the tomb day and night.

A few days later, some friends went to Jesus' tomb. The big stone was rolled away. "It's empty," they shouted when they looked in.

Then they saw an angel. "Jesus is not here," the angel said. "He is alive again!" So they ran to tell the others.

After Jesus rose from the dead, he visited his friends who were happy to see him. Before he left for heaven, he told them to spread the good news of God's love to everyone. Because Jesus died and rose again, he earned us a place in heaven. That's why we celebrate Easter.

Things to Know About Easter

We celebrate Easter to remember what Jesus did for us, and how much he loves us.

Because Jesus gave his life for us, and rose again, we can live again, too.

Easter comes on a Sunday in spring.

Spring is the season when grass grows, flowers bloom, and baby animals begin their new lives.

When we believe in Jesus, we have a new life, too.

Can you answer these questions?

1. What did Jesus ride when he came into Jerusalem?

2. What did Jesus give to his friends at the Last Supper?

3. Who turned Jesus over to the mean leaders?

4. What did the mean leaders ask Jesus at his trial?

5. What did some friends see when they came to Jesus' tomb?

Turn the page for the answers.